LET ME GET THIS OFF MY CHEST

-

COPING WITH BREAST CANCER ALONE

by JANICE MUIR

Copyright © 2020 Janice Muir
All rights reserved
Printed ISBN: 9780 9874011 6 8
E Pub E-Book ISBN 9780 987401182

Self Publishing via Ingram Spark

Graphic Design & Artwork
Astrid Kuenne (Your Brand Management)
www.yourbrandmanagement.com.au

janicemuir.com

LET ME GET THIS OFF MY CHEST
- COPING WITH BREAST CANCER ALONE by   JANICE MUIR

Let ME get this off MY chest – Coping with breast cancer Alone
© Jan Muir 2020

All rights reserved. No Part of this publication may be reproduced, stored in a retrieval system, or transmitted in any form or by any means, electronic, mechanical, photocopying, recording or otherwise, without the prior written permission of the author.

This book is designed to provide information and motivation to our readers. It is sold with the understanding that the publisher is not engaged to render any type of psychological, legal, or any other kind of professional advice. The content of this publication is the sole expression and opinion of its author. No warranties or guarantees are expressed or implied by the author or publisher's choice to include any of the content in this volume. Neither the publisher nor the individual author(s) shall be liable for any physical, psychological, emotional, financial, or commercial damages, including, but not limited to special incidental consequential or other damages. Our views and rights are the same: You are responsible for your own choices and actions and results.

National Library Of Australia Cataloguing-in-Publication (pbk)

Author: Muir, Jan, Author
Title: Let ME get this off MY chest / Janice Muir
ISBN: 9780 9874011 6 8 (paperback)
ISBN: 9780 987401182- (E-Book; E-Pub)
Subjects: Biography.
                Self-Help Techniques

Published by Janice Muir
Self-Published I Believe I Achieve

A Tribute To Jean Thomsen

Jean Thomsen came into my life when I was first diagnosed with Cancer, and for that I am ever so grateful. She comforted me during my journey in a way that no one else could.

You see she was an angel to me, and her spirit touched mine in a way that lifted my own spirits to get through.

She shared words of wisdom and comfort whenever we met. She knew of my struggles and she knew how to make me laugh when I was feeling low.

I never had the chance to say my goodbyes to Jean in person when her passing in life came.

I am forever grateful for this beautiful soul, a true blessing and dearly missed.

RIP Jean Thomsen
11 October 2017

Dedication

A friend I call my buddy, who stood by me through this ordeal. Who comforted me through this journey and truly became a remarkably close deep and caring companion.

Words cannot express my appreciation for everything you shared with me on this journey;

Thank you Vito De Marchi.

Endorsement

'An interesting insight into one woman's journey with Breast Cancer and what she went through on that journey'.

A good interesting story.

                    Carol Duggan

                    Proofreader

                    Shepparton, Victoria

LET ME GET THIS OFF MY CHEST ... viii
- COPING WITH BREAST CANCER ALONE *by* JANICE MUIR

Table of Contents

Forward xi
Acknowledgements xv
Introduction xxi
Chapter One 1
　Things Were Almost Normal Again
Chapter Two 9
　Until Everything Fell Apart
Chapter Three 17
　Just When it Couldn't Get Any Worse
Chapter Four 23
　The Scare
Chapter Five 31
　Coping With the Pressures
Chapter Six 41
　Bucket Load of Tears
Chapter Seven 53
　Self Sufficient
Chapter Eight 57
　Chemo Numbness Effect
Chapter Nine 65
　Finding Hope and Healing
Chapter Ten 75
　Mindset Awareness
Chapter Eleven 85
　Five Years Later – All Clear
Chapter Twelve 93
　Seven Outcomes
Let Me Get This Off My Chest 107
About Janice Muir 111

Forward

Jan and I met in Darwin over 35 years ago. We were both living and working there at the time. We had an instant connection and our friendship has remained strong since that time. She was a happy, full of life person that was always the glass half full, not half empty. She was robust and gregarious, and she had a way about her that attracted people to her and a sexiness that exuded from every pore.

When Jan's illness became her very survival, those wonderful qualities took a back seat. Only temporarily I'm happy to say.

The fight to live is one of the most powerful forces in the human body. Having an illness just makes that fight more worthwhile.

Jan fought the fight. She not only fought the fight, she basically fought it alone.

      And she won!

Its human nature to think that "it will never happen to me". Then one day it does happen to you and you realise how vulnerable you really are and at the same time, how precious life is. The decisions to be made from that time on are a game changer in anyone's life.

Jan's decision firstly to undergo the mastectomy and then the struggle to come to terms with losing a boob was probably at the time, the biggest blow to her as she suddenly felt less of a woman. Processing that in one's mind is unimaginable. They say time is a good healer, yet how long is time that heals those wounds, or at least allows you to live with them.

I remember getting phone calls at all hours of the night and day with Jan on the other end crying at her wits end – her hair was falling out or she couldn't drag herself up out of bed, or she just wanted to talk to someone and share the pain.

And she came through

Jan never wanted Chemo; she didn't want that pure poison in her body. So, struggling with this concept, she finally found a balance between having the chemo to keep alive, and assisting her body cope with the process by natural remedies. As with everything she does, Jan went into the research of both processes head on and with gusto. It was her body and she was having a say in what was going in and out of it. I believe she found a balance that she could work with.

Jan had to take stock of herself and her body. She had to find that inner strength to clear her head and make decisions she never thought she would have to make. It's a time when you really look at yourself and say, what do I want and what is best for me. Jan being the person who over analyses everything, would have analysed this until she was out of all scenarios and able to accept the most "liveable" scenario for herself.

This book is the endurance of being persistent and being determined to beat the disease that impacted Jan's life.

When I was reading it, I felt captivated and wanted to keep reading. Its shared lots of courage and other aspects about Jan that I know now is what got her through this illness.

Her guts and determination shared in this story is the courage and strength now going into the 15th year (at the time of publishing) being clear of cancer.

I now see a different woman. One that lives every day to the fullest, craves for learning new things, and is passionate about everything she does. She is once again robust and gregarious; she has a wicked sense of humour and is not afraid to share that humour around. She just brings things alive and its very contagious.

She went through a lot on her own and now she longs for quality time with her family and friends as she knows how precious life is and how quickly it can be cut short.

My friendship with Jan has endured the time and struggles and I hope from this day on that her troubles are less; her blessings are more and may nothing, but happiness come through her door.

I'm very proud of her intestinal fortitude and believe that she is what she is today because of it.

Love Lisa Syme-Cobb xx

Janice: My Best Ever Friend of over 35 years.

LET ME GET THIS OFF MY CHEST
- COPING WITH BREAST CANCER ALONE *by* JANICE MUIR

Acknowledgements

I had the pleasure of meeting Janice Muir some time ago now; and yet it was not until the past year that I became aware of her 'breast cancer' journey, and then only that there as a mention that she was going to purchase a new prosthesis.

Personally, I wasn't aware that she had one! In reading Janice's book 'LET ME GET THIS OFF MY CHEST – COPING WITH BREAST CANCER ALONE' by Janice Muir, I was both honored and grateful to be walking in some small way on Janice's journey with her. Yet even more grateful to her; for the other women who will take from those personal and yet profound words that she has shared, something that resonates for them. May Janice's words shine a light of hope for you.

Sheila Kennedy

Sydney

www.sheila-kennedy.com

I have had the privilege to read Janice Muir's book "Let Me Get This Off My Chest - Coping With Breast Cancer Alone". This is an awesome book – a very personal story. Janice opens her heart and shares her breast cancer journey. We are there with her at every step sharing her private thoughts, her triumphs, her challenges and her lessons.

I highly recommend reading this book. This book is not just about Janice and her story. What you take away from this book are brilliant lessons for life that everyone can apply.

I especially loved "the pivotal point of the push...". It was an out of the box event that had such a profound effect; read the book and see how small things can impact to produce major changes.

For me the book was summed up brilliantly in Chapter 12 where Janice brings her journey, her feelings, the events to a great conclusion that highlights the outstanding lessons she shares.

Trish Springsteen

Creative Business Consultant

www.trishspringsteen.com

Janice opens herself to share her raw and real story of coping with cancer alone, a journey of recovery and self-discovery as much as a triumphant life challenge and a true lesson in developing resilience. The outcomes she shares are invaluable for anyone traversing cancer and seeking to find that inner strength, fortitude and focus to not only survive but become a stronger, more focused human being. A great gift for those you love who need to learn from someone who has walked in their shoes.

Lauren Clemett

International Award Winner, Best-Selling Author

theaudaciousagency.com/

Hi Jan,

I have finished reading your book and thoroughly enjoyed it. I loved the way you kept it light but real so that we could understand and connect on various levels with your journey...your struggles, your mindset and your triumphs!

I could relate on many levels.

I lost my Mum to breast cancer (well at least that's where it started) in 2005. My Mum was a vibrant larger than life person who everyone loved with a great attitude to life.

Sadly, though she lived a very tough life growing up and had much emotional baggage which I feel contributed to her illness and sadly not surviving her 4-year Cancer journey.

Reading your book allowed me to relate more personally to her journey and what she may have gone through. I recall her dislike of the color 'Purple' because of the Chemo room having everything in Purple!

I lived in a different State when she went through much of her treatments and only moved to join her in Qld a few short months before she passed away at only 62 years young (3 years older than I am currently at 59).

I TOTALLY believe that we play a HUGE part in our health and wellness journey in the choices that we make and the way that we think.

I believe that having Gratitude for our health, wellness, our financial situation, our relationships and all that comes to us in life plays a HUGE part.

So, thank you for allowing me to be a part of your story.

Reading it further strengthened in my mind that I do have a say in what happens to thoughts, by the choices I make and the thoughts, I think.

I choose vibrant health and a positive mindset.

Cheers! Lillian

Lillian Reekie

Freedom Warrior

lillian@thefreedomwarrior.com.au

LET ME GET THIS OFF MY CHEST
- COPING WITH BREAST CANCER ALONE *by* JANICE MUIR

... xx

Introduction

> *"There is a saying in Tibetan, 'Tragedy should be utilized as a source of strength.' No matter what sort of difficulties, how painful the experience is, if we lose our hope, that's our real disaster."*
>
> – Dalai Lama

Nothing prepares you for the tragedy that comes around occasionally because of just being alive. Research is conducted frequently on the illnesses and diseases that afflict the human body. Findings are broadcast across several media platforms to educate and enlighten the public about them; however, it still seems so far away and unlikely that it would ever happen to you.

This denial keeps you going and usually forms a wall of protection around you, as you make strides and achieve goals in your life. You begin to feel almost invincible. If you wake up feeling just fine, nothing could possibly go wrong.

Research on breast cancer shows that the risk of developing breast cancer increases with age. In Australia, studies have found that an average of fifty-three women are diagnosed with breast cancer daily. This could sound alarming and you might be thrown aback by this statistic.

The reality is that many of the women who are diagnosed with breast cancer, felt just fine until that care-free brush of their arms against one of their breasts causing discomfort and or pain. For others, it could be a visit to the doctor which should just be a routine breast exam. Routine, because, that is what the reports and findings urge us all to do to be sure nothing's sneaking up on you. I doubt that anyone would hope to find something wrong during a routine exam.

During my battle with cancer, I occasionally wondered how different it might've been if I ate more nutritious meals, slept better, relaxed more often and so on. Most of the time, I had no answers at all. There is always the chance that regardless of measures taken to stave off the onset of breast cancer, it could still sneak up on you.

We don't know what we don't know until we are faced with the experience. I was to be faced with so many unknown events it changed my life.

At forty-seven, I believed I still had many productive years ahead in my life. I had dreams, hopes and aspirations I still wanted to fulfil, and I was certain that achieving

them was very possible. Life hadn't been a bed of roses or without downsides. Don't get me wrong! I felt like I was way on top of every situation that I would encounter so long as I remained positive and did what I could, by way of working continuously to achieve the goals I set.

There are no satisfying words that can completely describe the way everything comes crashing down when you hear the big "C" word. Emotionally and mentally the impact you feel inside is indescribable. It hits you at the core of your being. I didn't want to believe what I was being told. STUNNED! Describes it best.

Studies that state the different reactions, observed in different women, from various cultures, try to group these reactions into chunks that can then be written out and dished out as descriptions. None of these categories and chunks of description can portray the fear that suddenly grips one's heart or the aloneness that one is enveloped with when faced with the news of a diagnosis. For me, it was a shock unlike any I had ever felt before! Every time I recall that moment, it still sends shivers down my spine.

Surviving breast cancer is for some, one of the bravest things that they have ever done in their whole lives. There is no manual for survival except taking all the treatment that is recommended and hoping to the high heavens that it all works out for the better. That's it! You just never really know if it will work, however best to believe that it can.

Breast Cancer demands the most from the women who are diagnosed with it and nothing ever returns to normal after that. Finding the resilience that you may not be aware that you are even capable of having, becomes the real saviour. There are many personal reports from women who try to describe the pain they felt while receiving treatment. Sharing how the only solace they could find, even though they were surrounded by family and friends, was in their ability and courage to see things through to the very end, no matter how fatal it might be. Yet always taking one day at a time.

In this book, I share the most wrenching periods of my adult life while battling cancer and the hope I found amid the pain and despair that was my constant companion. My journey is truly unique to me. It also shares my link to every other woman who is living through breast cancer or is a survivor.

One of the most uplifting moments in my fight against breast cancer was when I could connect with someone else. Someone who had been through this pain, or was going through this pain, and could understand the way it all felt. Although I went through the process of treatment mostly alone because my family could not always be present, I felt warmed and grateful for the new connections and friendships I developed along my path to recovery.

As I stated earlier, life is never the same after you've come out of the "C" woods. I have learned that this does not have to be a terrible thing for us warriors. The experience is forever etched in our subconscious and try as we might to deny this fact, it shapes our reality from that moment onwards. It took a great deal of willpower, openness and courage to take a shot at beating the odds.

On my path, there were moments where I was uncertain that I could continue this fight, however I stayed on regardless. Amid the doubts that kept surfacing as to the efficacy of the treatments I received, I trudged on, slowly wedging those doubts out and replacing them with positive thoughts.

A key lesson for me remains that the outcome of life is mostly uncertain no matter how much we want to believe that we know the way things will pan out in the near or far future. The best approach in the face of this great uncertainty is cultivating a brave spirit and a positive mindset. Being alone for most of my treatment, I had to be strong for myself and this saved me from slowly sinking into depression. Doing that would've made matters worse for me.

In this book, you will find the various therapies that I constantly took to help my recovery process through chemotherapy. I will also highlight the various strengths and weaknesses of some of these therapies and treatment procedures that I took. It is a tell-all book and even as I type these words, I cannot know for certain how much it will impact or affect the way you see things. As with all things uncertain in life, I have chosen to bravely share my experience with you and my hope is that you will find one or more things that you will relate with and which forms a part of your experience of life.

Hints and Tips

- Have regular checks with Doctor;
- Know your own breast, handle them with care; Know the contours and structure of the breast; A hard lump is easy to detect – it's like a hard-frozen pea; - Its HARD;
- Keep your body 80% Alkaline and 20% Acidic;
- Google 80% Alkaline 20% Acidic.

Resource: store.nutritionalresources.com/products/80-20-alkaline-acid-foods-chart

LET ME GET THIS OFF MY CHEST
- COPING WITH BREAST CANCER ALONE *by* JANICE MUIR

Chapter One

Always according to where we place our thoughts, do we gain the result. This is Law.

— Paramananda

Things Were Almost Normal Again

Moving to Brisbane in 2001 came in the wake of having made the decision to allow my partner into an assisted living facility for people living with Alzheimer's. Making the decision in a way that would be best for my daughter, my partner and I was a very tough one. However, once made, I knew I had made the right choice for my daughter and me to move on.

Providing care and support for my partner took a toll on my emotions and this affected my relationship with my daughter to a great extent. Looking back now, I would say that I acted as though I was the only person losing someone dear to them when in fact, my daughter was too.

The consequences of this detachment from my daughter at a crucial point in our lives resulted in an estrangement at a time where we should have banded even closer together. So, while I moved to Brisbane, my daughter picked Darwin as a place to settle; a thirty-eight-hour drive or five-hour flight apart.

I moved into an apartment that was best suited for one person while I focused on being able to secure a permanent job for myself. I wasn't really the kind of person that had everything figured out for themselves. I usually took things a day at a time and this was the case in Brisbane. I worked long hours and took short breaks in-between. I tried to eat healthy, but I cannot really say that I made as much effort to keep up this healthy eating style due to the nature of my work.

A typical day would have me waking up at five am to get on the train at six so I could be at work by seven am. At work, I'd be on the go with a short break in between until about four pm and then I'd head home. Usually, I'd be home by 5:30 pm on good days. The short breaks in between might've passed unnoticed because I often worked through my lunchtime, grabbing a bite here or there.

Without a well-defined long-term plan, while moving in 2001, I went along with a simple plan that revolved around finding a stable, permanent source of income at the very least and then making up more plans as I go along. In all, I was learning new things about Brisbane, finding my way around the city and making new connections with people.

Dating was high on my list of things to become engaged in and even with this too, I took things as they came along. I would say that I did not really pursue it with as intense an effort as I did with obtaining a permanent job placement. The housing unit I'd moved into wasn't in the classiest areas in town, but it was in a secure area and I was glad to have a roof over my head at the very least. I also had hopes that things were bound to change for the better now that I was starting out again in a new place where possibilities were rife.

The rest of my family was in Melbourne and we chatted over long and short calls occasionally. For the most part, I was on my own. I didn't really mind this much because I have a very independent mindset. This is coupled with the fact that while growing up, I believed in the notion that life starts at forty. I believed that I still had plenty of time on my hands to travel to places I'd always wanted to see and ride the most perfect car; it didn't feel like I was missing out on anything by being alone at forty-seven.

Sewing is my most relaxing activity and other times when I felt like doing more upbeat things over the weekend, I'd hang out with a friend at a coffee shop and just chat.

I was coasting mostly. My life wasn't in the best of places and I was sure that with the right amount of effort as I put in finding a permanent source of income, I could become open to more adventures. So, I was doing just fine were my thoughts.

In 2005 however, I had a small problem. I noticed that I was spot bleeding in between my periods, and I went to see a specialist. While there, they confirmed that I had something they called, pre-cervical cancer as I recall. I needed to have a good part of my cervix removed. It was good that I had found this out and consulted a specialist even though it wasn't posing so much of a health problem at the time. To my thinking it wasn't a big deal at all and once the procedure was completed, I was cleared of the pre-cervical cancer diagnosis and so, I skipped on along on life's pathway.

During this time, I started taking personal development classes and became more interested in getting good quality products; food and otherwise. I started studying the use of good quality products to improve my overall wellbeing and implemented some changes in my existing diet, however not extensively.

As I grew older, I'd always hoped that I could see my grandchildren and be surrounded by family as I aged. This hope was dashed with the slow deterioration of my partner's health when he was diagnosed with Alzheimer's. Taking care of him was a most intense emotional period

for me and even though after his placement in a home I had moved to Brisbane and was slowly letting go of the emotional trauma. I'd say that some of it still lingered as it took a while getting used to living alone again as I did not have a lot of options at that time.

A part of me longed to reconnect more meaningfully with my daughter again yet with the distance, (she was in Darwin) I wasn't sure this would go very smoothly. The trauma she had passed through and the way she handled it was still a sore spot for us both. As time passed, I could not see the need in trying to put any blame on anything. Let alone factor that the cause of the rift between my daughter and myself had occurred in the past nor could I block out the reality that there was a rift between my daughter and me.

In the period where her dad struggled with Alzheimer's, she became increasingly involved in unsavoury company and being only in her mid-teens, she was really at the wild youthful age. Sometimes, I wonder how different things would've been if I had opted to multitask a little by showing my daughter that I was still there for her, even though her father was declining. We could make the most of it all and grow stronger together. Life did what it did. Whilst it caused some tension it was in the past of life, where lessons were learned, and experiences were a part of this period.

I was slowly coming to terms with how wrapped up in my emotions I had been at the time, thus causing me to neglect my dearest daughter's emotional needs. Coming to terms with this fact encouraged my extra effort into working at building a relationship with my daughter that could work and then, going from there to becoming even more involved in her life. Something that I'd always longed for.

These were my plans as the year 2006 started. I'd now been in Brisbane for five years and regardless of how populous it was, I was finding my place in it. Earlier, I stated that allowing my partner to enter an assisted nursing home was one of the most suited decisions to make at the time. Looking back now, I know that if I had carried on being the sole provider of care and support for my partner, I would've caved due to the emotional burden of it all. Let alone losing my home and financial status would have had a different circumstance for life.

As I made the decision, I trusted that I still had a chance to heal from that trying period in my life. I think that my strength and courage lay in holding on to hope and working towards achieving more daily. I might've been alone in Brisbane, yet I might as well have had a squadron backing me up because that is what my courage and resilience felt like for me.

Unexpectantly then everything falls apart!

Hints and Tips

- Keep your communication open with your children; Let them grow by the experiences;
- Honour yourself with small treats and things you can really benefit from not because from the sake of having it;
- Keep the main thing the main thing so you do the main thing for yourself – Honour yourself.

LET ME GET THIS OFF MY CHEST
- COPING WITH BREAST CANCER ALONE *by* JANICE MUIR

Chapter Two

Help if you can, if you cannot, fold your hands, standby and see where things go on.

– Swam Vivekanana

Until Everything Fell Apart

When you hear that you have a terminal illness, studies have shown that the knee-jerk response at first is instant denial. When the terminal illness has no symptoms that are immediately visible, the denial is even deeper. Research has highlighted that for some, their pattern of denial helps them get through their illness while for others, it could be detrimental.

In my case, my short-term denial helped me adjust slowly to the news of my diagnosis. Earlier in the month, I had observed what felt like hardness or a lump in my right breast and had gone to a specialist to have a breast exam and X-ray completed. It passed uneventfully and I was told that it may not be more than mastitis. At the mention of mastitis, I wondered to myself. I haven't had to breastfeed a baby in a long time so where would the mastitis be coming from. This thought did not last long on my mind as I shrugged it off as nothing and I carried on with my activities the next day and the day after that.

I got a call from the hospital a few days later that was marked urgent and demanded a visit within twenty-four hours of receiving the message. It said I needed to complete a biopsy exam as a follow-up on my initial visit. This did not ring any alarm bells at the time as I thought it was merely a performance of due diligence on the part of the professionals.

I went in for the appointment on the 19th of April taking some time off work to quickly get it done. Getting there, the nurse attendant told me as she prepared me for the procedure that it'll all be over soon. I did not think so much about her statement until I was lying on the table in the procedure room for the biopsy. It turns out she was saying those words to calm me as the procedure turned out to involve more than I thought it initially would.

The biopsy made me tense and with the fact that they said I should lie so still throughout the process; it was all I could do to stay put for the whole process. I started hyperventilating however when they brought out what looked like a big yarn needle and wanted to insert it into a side of my right breast. I later found that this was the biopsy needle and that the discomfort I felt as they inserted it was a very common feeling. The procedure lasted a long time. They kept saying something about not being able to get at the tissue. They were trying to collect from the right angle, hence the prolonged nature of the procedure.

I was still not alarmed at this point and it isn't unlikely that you are thinking of me as a much-uninvolved person right now. I was deeply uninvolved in the process and you could say that perhaps I thought myself invincible. There were some tell-tale signs here after all and as they ushered me into the waiting room, my mind fleeted to the last time I had come in for the X-rays. The radiologist had told me that it'll be fine, and that the good thing was that I was in a good hospital and they'd take care of me. I shrugged at the memory recall, still not suspecting that anything could be amiss. The biopsy insertion point turned into a bruise and even though the nurses said it would clear up after a few days, I still felt some measure of discomfort as I left the procedure room.

The wait for the biopsy results turned into a long one, lasting about four hours and within this time, I had to call in at work to keep them up to date on the visit to the hospital. By the time I was called in to see the doctor, it was already late in the afternoon and work was almost closing. He ushered me into his office and proceeded to place my X-ray results on the viewer in his office. At this point, the professional and detached demeanour I observed in the doctor was starting to make me apprehensive yet, never once did the thought of a breast cancer diagnosis cross my mind.

As I stared at the X-rays, they looked normal to me although there was some glow, I noticed in some areas that seemed a little off to me. The doctor started up by saying that there was no easy way to break the news that he was about to, and I remember cutting him off and asking him to kindly explain what he had on the screen as my X-ray results. He seemed startled by the curt way I cut him off, yet I know that his startled state was nothing compared to the apprehension that had now grown to monumental proportions inside of me. This was something unusual and it seemed to me that the doctor wanted this to drag on while all I really just wanted was to get this over with as I had already lost most of my day sitting and waiting for the results from the biopsy exam.

I did not want to voice my apprehension and state that I wasn't feeling ill and as such did not understand what all the delay was. I was very near to that point when I cut the doctor off and asked that he tell me what news there was. Well, he certainly took my advice and gave me the news straight. He told me that based on the biopsy test results and with the observations of my x-rays, I had been diagnosed with breast cancer.

It seemed wrong to me that those words could flow freely through the doctor's lips when he was not inside of my body. I felt fine and I wasn't sure he knew that I felt just fine. I needed to tell him that I did not feel like I had cancer at all. I walked into the hospital myself. How many people living with cancer could do that?

Something inside me screamed denial. The doctor did not know what he was saying to me. How could he? He only had tests and test results are wrong all the time, right? Maybe there was a mix-up somewhere and this will all be cleared up quickly. These thoughts overwhelmed me and even though I did not voice them all, the doctor must've noticed because he gave me some minutes to breathe and collect myself before I could voice my first question. What do you mean by I have breast cancer?

He proceeded to explain the observations they made and the conclusions they had drawn. The X-ray showed that I had three lumps in my right breast. This new relevant piece of information floored me even more. Three lumps?! In one breast?

He continued to explain that one of the lumps was 2cm in length which was consistent with aggressive stage four while the other two were 1 cm each, consistent with stage three. This measurement was just the length and its girth hadn't yet been ascertained at that point and so the actual size of each lump was still unknown.

I was overwhelmed by all this information coming at me so fast to say the very least. It still didn't make sense to me that I felt fine and even healthy and yet I had not one, but three cancerous lumps growing in my right breast. It was very tempting to go on denying this news, but I could not help but piece things together gradually.

The X-rays had my name on them and now, I knew what the glow I had noticed earlier stood for. I could not help however also recall the radiologist's words to me when I got the results on my first visit to the hospital. It all made sense now and I could go on denying it, yet of what use will that be? The surgeon who broke the news to me couldn't just be playing a prank on me. He's too busy trying to save lives to play pranks.

I felt so lonely as they ushered me out of the office and into the waiting area, I had been sitting in some minutes ago. Even amid the hustle and movement around me, I felt very isolated from my environment. I pondered my options at fighting cancer and kept coming up with blanks. I was alone in Brisbane without a lot of close female friends to speak of.

One of my sisters lived in Brisbane and she had her own family and wouldn't possibly be able to drop all that and come stay with me. I wouldn't even want her to sacrifice that much for me. I was alone in every sense of the word and try as I might, I could not shake off the anger that welled up inside me at having to battle breast cancer and take care of myself alone even after I had been there for my partner as and when he was diagnosed with Alzheimer's Dementia.

Hints and Tips

- Never put off till tomorrow what you can do today;
- Your action may save your life;
- Your body gives you signs; acknowledge them;
- Tomorrow maybe too late;
- The voice inside your head is your guide;
- Listen and ACT on what is being said to you.

Chapter Three

Your heart knows in silence the secrets of the days and nights, but your ears thirst for the sound of your heart's knowledge.

– Kahlil Gibran

Just When it Couldn't Get Any Worse

Before moving to Brisbane and making plans to allow my partner into a nursing facility for people living with Alzheimer's, I was my partner's sole caregiver. Typically, in a relationship or marriage, both parties take care of each other's needs and the roles are constantly alternating between both parties.

When one of the two parties involved is diagnosed with a terminal or debilitating illness such as Alzheimer's, the roles tend to change. In the early stages, the role change isn't so drastic. Things can still be described as almost normal. As the disease progresses, the roles are switched fully, and it begins to resemble the relationship of a parent and her child instead of that of a partnership or life-long friendship between two healthy individuals.

One partner becomes solely responsible for the other. When things are not happening the way they usually do, it is a cause for alarm. Maybe he hasn't come home at the usual time he returns from the walk he takes in the evenings. You cannot help but wonder if he's late because he met a friend on the road and is catching up on the latest gossip or news in the neighbourhood or if he simply lost his way because he cannot remember the way that leads back home. The emotional trauma is crippling.

Reports from several marriages that are ripped in half by the diagnosis of one spouse with Alzheimer's are manifold. When these partners living with Alzheimer's are especially scarred by the diagnosis because of its implications on their overall well-being and lifestyle, it takes an even greater toll on the caregiver. Maybe the partner living with Alzheimer's is so used to doing things by himself (or by herself) and doing them excellently and is suddenly

requiring aid to complete even the simplest tasks because the hard-wired ability and memories are simply not there anymore. It can be very disheartening seeing all of this unfold and the reactions are never pleasant.

My partner became a stranger as his condition deteriorated. Observing all of this happen while I could only watch helplessly was the most terrifying experience I'd ever had until that point in my life. This was my partner, the one I'd planned to spend the rest of my life with and whom I had built so much emotion and so much of my life around. Watching the changes that started in him and never really having any way to wrap my head around them caused many negative emotions to well up inside of me. I knew he wasn't changing of his own accord and that if he had a say in all of this, he'd choose to not change so drastically but it did not change the fact that I was helpless.

Providing care and support through this period in our lives was very stressful for me. Taking care of my partner had to be a full-time job however I combined it with my regular jobs still. It is often a wonder to me how I did not cave in early or give in to the negative emotions that often welled up inside me when I'd get a negative response from my partner for something I was trying to help him with; something he'd usually appreciate that I helped him do if he was himself.

That's right. My partner wasn't himself anymore and I struggled with the decision to let him get better care from people who would be devoted to taking care of him without having so much expectation from him as I evidently did, even though I knew that it would be futile to expect anything of him. It was hard for me to take care of matters around the house in addition to taking care of my spouse when these were tasks that we usually just split between each other. By the time I took the courage to accept help and let him go into the facility, I was sure that I had reached my wit's end.

There are a lot of reports of people feeling guilty about letting their spouses go and how it feels like they are deserting their partners. It felt this way for me for a while and as I decided to move to Brisbane to start out again, I knew deeply that I had done my best and that my partner will be better cared for in a place specializing in that kind of care.

Letting him go was a good decision for me to make and even as I look back on how long it took me to reach that decision, I knew the reasons I had held on for so long and I knew that no one could fault me for wanting and needing to be there for my partner through those difficult times. Providing care for him took its toll on my body, yet I did not want to have it any other way than the way it happened. My world changed again April 20th, 2006.

Hints and Tips

- Things happen in life for many reasons, I believe to teach us life lessons on the many areas of life that happen to us for us to grow;

- Be very mindful of everything that happens in life to you, for you, about you and around you. Take what you need to move forward with conviction and follow through.

LET ME GET THIS OFF MY CHEST
- COPING WITH BREAST CANCER ALONE *by* JANICE MUIR   ... 22

Chapter Four

There is no ladder to climb; there is only the first steps; and the first step is to the everlasting step.

– Krishnamurti

The Scare

The stories I'd heard about breast cancer patients were not very pleasant ones. Most of the time, it was about the pain and depression associated with the treatments that ensued shortly after the diagnosis. The most unpleasant part of the whole situation was the uncertainty of the outcomes expected down the line. There were no sure hopes that after this and that treatment, the cancer will be gone forever. If not, then my days were numbered, and I needed to fight hard.

As I sat at the waiting area again after receiving the news of the diagnosis, these thoughts filled my head as I pondered my next steps. I could not help and wonder what was happening to me and at this age. I never really recalled saying why me. I wanted to live up to fifty and beyond. Fifty was only 2 yrs away and I wanted longer than two years. I needed to do so much more in the world around me. Maybe I hadn't gotten around to doing that much up till this point, yet I was always hopeful, that I could get a chance to be more impactful to my environment.

I was actively working towards reaching that point. I tried very hard to shake off the images of my body being enclosed in a box and the box being lowered into a six-foot deep hole however to no avail. My life, as I saw it, might just be over right now and I don't have much to show for it.

The news that I had breast cancer was not something that I could have ever envisaged would come around and certainly not in the sudden way that it did. I was unprepared for this. I had no one to care for me. I knew I would need to be cared for in the coming months as I started my treatment. I kept thinking to myself, what do I do now? How can I cope with this while living alone? Who could I turn to for support? I was stumped internally with this; - It was not a good feeling for me.

When I was ushered out of the surgeon's office, still dazed from the news, I was handed over to a volunteer assistant who was supposed to console me and offer some immediate support after getting the news of my diagnosis. The kind of decisions I would make, the help I would need to think straight and clearly would be offered to me by this volunteer and I remember wondering to myself how this stranger could possibly help me out. Little did I know!

I wondered how anyone expected me to listen to what a stranger had to say to me about the news that had just altered my entire life. If I wasn't so overwhelmed and shocked at the news, I might've been amused by the fact that the hospital that appointed this volunteer, felt they could be of any help to newly diagnosed patients when they were complete strangers to them.

It turns out I was wrong about my assumptions about this lady volunteer. As I would find out later my subsequent visits to the hospital, she was a breast cancer survivor and had been volunteering at the hospital to aid women newly diagnosed with breast cancer through the first few chaotic hours of their diagnosis. If I wasn't so distracted by the weight of my diagnosis, I might've been able to infer that she must've been through this herself or have been through it with someone dear to her going by how empathic and understanding she was as I sat down with her.

I could not make out most of the words she said to me as I wrapped in the cocoon of numbness that I felt from my neck downwards. It felt like my body parts had stopped working upon hearing the news, even though it was all mostly in my head and not very real. The volunteer Mez stayed with me through my turmoil and gradually, her words began to register in my conscious thoughts. She was asking me questions that started registering as practical to me. Who could I call to come around? Where was my family? Were there any calls she could help me make at that point?

These questions made the situation I was in dawn on me even more and terrifying as it was, I had to start accepting the reality. I knew that even though I had family that I could call, I was still essentially alone and for starters, I'd have to drive myself back home that day in peak hour traffic. The questions helped clear my mind a little bit and the next thoughts that settled in my mind were that I could not possibly call anyone with this news. They'd be thoroughly devastated. I did not even know the words to say to break the news to them.

Breaking the news to my daughter worried me the most because I could not help or recall at that moment, the pain that she had gone through when her father was diagnosed with Alzheimer's. Knowing that I could potentially be lost to her as well seemed to me as too much for her to bear, as

she tried to piece her life together in Darwin. I simply did not have it in me to break this fatal news to her; not while I was still coming to terms with the fact myself.

Mez opted to call her up and inform her but I told her that I would do it soon. I just needed to gather enough courage to do so. I picked up the phone several times to make the call and still chickened out just before I hit the dial button. I just could not do it even though I realized deep down that I had to tell at least one person before leaving the hospital.

There were many more decisions that I needed to make at that point. I had already been scheduled for an appointment in three days and yet, all I could think of was running away from it all. Maybe as I drove home in peak hour traffic, someone would call from the hospital and tell me that it was all a mistake and that I did not need to come in after three days. The chances of that thought becoming reality were slim and I knew this even as those unlikely thoughts crossed my mind.

I made the calls eventually, hard as it was. I called my best girlfriend whom I go way back with and as I relayed the news to her, I burst into tears and by the time the call had ended, she too was crying on the other end. This was the trend for me with the calls I made from the hospital and I knew that I had more hard calls to make upon getting home from the hospital.

It did not seem wise to me to call the office with the news from the hospital. I just managed to call and tell them that I had to stay longer at the hospital and as such, it would not be possible to head back to work since it was already late. I told them I'd be in the next day and as I ended the call, I wondered how I could hold onto that job when I became too ill to work.

By the time these few calls had been made, I had regained a semblance of control over my emotions. With the help and steady guidance from Mez, I was beginning to think more practically. I needed to break the news to more members of my family and to my partner at this time, but I decided to wait until I got home before making those calls. This particular Wednesday was indeed the toughest day I'd had in the recent past and I cannot say where I drew most of my strength from to maintain my composure for the few hours I stayed in the hospital after the news of my diagnosis.

Somewhere deep in my subconscious, I knew I had to find a way to fight this condition I had been diagnosed with. I knew I could not give in too easily even though it didn't seem to me like I could weather the pressures of the coming months. I had to find a way to cope and deal with this alone because I knew I could not burden my family and my daughter with the sole task of taking care of me.

I know the effect it had on me as I took care of my partner alone when he was diagnosed with Alzheimer's. I did not want to have anyone go through that much stress and pressure on my account. If I had anything that I could do to aid everyone around me in their process of helping me through this and myself as well, I wanted to be able to do just that.

This mindset that I was struggling to maintain as I drove out of the hospital that day would serve to be my solace for the gruelling months of treatment that ensued. This mindset filled me with courage when I struggled with bouts of despair and it has since altered how much I believe in my ability to persevere through dire circumstances. You'll find in the next chapters, the effects of the treatment that was recommended for my care on my emotional, physical and psychological well-being. In these chapters, I walk you through every phase of my treatment; the triumphs as well as the trials I witnessed along my journey.

Hints and Tips

- Everything you need comes from within;
- Trust your inner being to know the way;
- Ask yourself the question; What is the next thing I do to move forward – see where it leads you;
- Questions you ask your self are the answers to move forward - Trust they will guide you.

Chapter Five

It's not the load that breaks you down, it's the way you carry it.

– Lou Holtz

Coping With the Pressures

At the beginning of this book, I pointed out that nothing prepares anyone for the tragedy that comes around in their lives. Being diagnosed with breast cancer hit me hard and it took all my willpower to pick up the courage to choose to fight the disease. My grandmother, as recounted by my mother, had been diagnosed at the age of fifty-two and so, you can imagine my dismay at getting it so much earlier and even more so when my mother was diagnosed at the age of seventy-two.

My family, on my mother's side, has a history of breast cancer. I remember when I was as young as three years old. There was a period where my mother was frequenting the hospital and an event where I witnessed her crying uncontrollably and it wasn't until later, that I learned that my mom lost her mom to breast cancer around that time.

I remember my mum recounting to me how much the illness affected her mom. Watching her mum's health decline slowly had deeply affected her and pushed her towards taking strict steps to prevent its occurrence in her and possibly, her three girls.

I remember being told when I was around twelve or thirteen years of age that the BRCA gene runs in our family and that there was a chance that my mom or anyone of us three girls would be diagnosed with it at some point in our lives. I never really gave it so much thought as you would expect. I was smart enough to throw words around as the intelligent teenager I was however, I wasn't smart enough then to completely internalize the implications of having the BRCA gene as part of my genetic makeup, nor did I realise the implications this gene in the body could do.

BRCA Gene[1] (positive) means you have a mutation in one of the breast cancer genes. My grandmother passed of Breast Cancer in the early 60's, I was diagnosed in 2006, then my mother in 2007.

---

1 BRCA: www.NationalBreastCancer.org

The more interesting angle to the way I dealt with having been told that I could potentially be diagnosed, even as I grew older, was that I was more inclined to believe that it'll be in my later years and since my grandmother did not have it until she was fifty-two. I still had time to live a full life. So, I very much looked forward to a full fifty years before worrying about what could hit me next.

This mindset is mostly the basis, in my opinion, for all my reactions to the news from my doctor. I just could not see it coming so early. It made no logical sense! All I could think of was how much I really wanted to see fifty and beyond. In that instant, I thought how much I really wanted to stay alive and see more of the world. I just wasn't ready to die yet. This could not be happening to me.

After I had broken the news of my diagnosis to my family, while on the phone with my mother on one of the subsequent days, she told me how sorry she was that it was me who was diagnosed with breast cancer so early while she, older as she was, was yet to be diagnosed. She was, however, diagnosed thirteen months and eleven days after my diagnosis and when she called me with the news of her diagnosis, she recounted how she already started suspecting that she too would be diagnosed soon after mine.

Our mindset and the things we say to self-have a huge impact on the outcomes in life. My mother's words floored me at the time when she shared "it was only a matter of time before I got cancer." Wow those words really hit home as to what we think about we bring about we create. I live in a healthy body has been my mantra through cancer and especially since the witness of secondary cancer with mum. Mum had around 6-8yrs clear, then secondary breast cancer was found in her lungs. She never recovered after 2 yrs of coping, passing 31st Oct 2018.

Looking back, I realize that it did not matter how prepared or devoted to staving off the onset of breast cancer. The news would still have floored me (and I'm sure it'll floor anyone). Even though my reactions are not ones that I am proud of having because they were just so disorganized and without direction, I have come to terms with the fact that, for someone without a manual (even with pamphlets that are supposed to be loaded with information), I was pretty composed afterwards.

Getting home from the hospital, I needed to lie down and clear my head, but I found that even this was a really difficult task to complete. I struggled and could not get over the sudden feeling of being unhealthy. Once I heard the news of having breast cancer, I felt like all my important organs had stopped functioning. Looking back, I can tell you that this is the point I started realizing that the mind is a very powerful tool.

I decided to call the rest of my family and break the news to them that afternoon. My sister worked close by to where I lived so I called her first. I told her that I had some important news to break to her in person, that I also needed to tell our parents and I'd want us to do it together. The way I said this must've alarmed her because she kept giving me searching glances when she came around to my house as I dialled our parents' number.

I broke the news to them shortly after they picked up and the look of shock, I saw on my sister's face was one that I was sure would mirror my parents' own. It was a shock for everyone who heard it and it was so because no one saw it coming at this stage of my life. The next words that ensued as the call unfolded, however, took me by surprise; even though looking back now, I cannot say that anyone could have known the right thing to say to me at that point.

I know now that the words they said to me about being strong enough to cope and having the capacity to get through this ordeal were all said in good faith. Those words were only meant to make me feel inspired and motivated enough to keep forging ahead. It didn't feel that way at the time, however, and I have chalked it up to the rawness of the emotions that still assuaged me at the news of my diagnosis. I felt like the words they were telling me about being strong enough to cope were just inappropriate. I felt this way so much so that I hung up in the middle of the call as though something else had cut the line off. It was just too emotionally intense for me.

I was feeling so hurt inside, yet something said I had to deal with this.

As I fumed, I wanted to shout at someone, throw something and yet, I knew that I had to be calm and remain that way no matter the pressures. I didn't know exactly what it was that I expected my parents to say about my diagnosis, however being told the obvious advice about needing to remain strong and resilient through it all did not help my emotions at all.

Inside of me I was screaming for compassion, gentle calming and encouraging words. Not the advice your strong enough to get through this. Not what I thought was a mother's love to attend to her eldest daughter. I was very numb with my news of diagnosis, these words only added to my pain.

Statements made in good faith or not, it just wasn't working for me and as I called them back, I resolved that I had to just refrain from increasing my expectation from people. No one can ever really read my mind and tell me the words I want to hear. Sure, they wanted to help as much as they could, where they could yet, I had to really come to terms with the fact that in the struggle against this cancer that was threatening to consume my right breast, I must make that entire journey alone. No amount of words from the people around me can serve to change this reality.

It was a disheartening situation for me, and it was the first step, as I would come to realize, towards taking full charge of my situation. I realized that it did not have to be an angry process for me, filled with negative emotions and getting annoyed when I wasn't being told what I felt like I needed to hear. I wanted to be able to accept aid when it was given and trudge on if it wasn't present. So, I resolved to carry on like this; wedging out the negativity that crept up every so often and replacing them with positive thoughts and just being appreciative wherever I was met with kind gestures. Deep at my core, I felt lost and resentment, yet underneath it all I also found resilience to keep going, not giving up.

This was not an easy path to decide to follow. I swayed to and from my decision. Each phase of the steps were also the steps of the emotions welling up massively from within. I witnessed this often in the early weeks after my diagnosis. Each time I swayed; I made a point to take myself back to that place where I was wedging the negativity out again. And so, back and forth, I kept going as the days passed by and I readied myself for the rounds of treatments that were coming.

There was a point when I was stuck in a vortex and I had myself buried 6 foot down. Not a very pleasant space when you know 3 breast cancer lumps are in the body. Losing a part of a body from an accident is horrific, deciding to cut a part of the body was no easy task. Three weeks later the decision was imminent. I was back in control of my body.

Despite that fact that I had had oodles and oodles of tears! I had come to a decision.

Hints and Tips

- What we think about we bring about. The mind is a powerful tool. Keep your thoughts on the outcomes you want in life;

- Negative thoughts will creep in – use the word 'Cancel' to remove them immediately.

LET ME GET THIS OFF MY CHEST
- COPING WITH BREAST CANCER ALONE *by* JANICE MUIR

Chapter Six

Live every second in the consciousness that you are immortal, thoughts and habits change; only your soul will be forever.

– Paramahansa Yogananda

Bucket Load of Tears

The moves for treatment commenced in earnest as I was scheduled for a follow-up appointment three days after my diagnosis. The pamphlets I'd been given were supposed to inform me about the course to follow as I was supposed to decide on either getting a lumpectomy or a mastectomy. This was perhaps the most difficult decision I have ever made in my entire life and it took me a long time to come to terms with first, my diagnosis and then the most suitable course of treatment to adopt.

As my denial slowly waned and I was still faced with the reality of living with cancer, a part of me still raged and railed at the universe or whatever force it was that guided the course of life. Often, I'd find myself wondering at how much I needed someone to be there for me like I had been for my partner and anger would well up inside of me at the thought of coping alone and fighting it all alone.

A part of me wanted to be able to share the pain as vividly as it occurred in my body with someone else. Most of the feedback I received from my family had been that I was strong, and I would cope just fine. Even though I knew deep down in my heart that I had to be strong for myself, I wished so intensely that it did not have to be so and that people didn't always have to say that it is possible to be that strong.

Before I made the decision on what procedure to adopt, I might as well have killed myself with all the time I spent making up my mind. It was a lot to stomach all too soon, but every minute I spent brooding and grieving internally, there was a greater chance that the cancer could become [2]metastatic seeing as the first lump was already in aggressive stage four. The hospital was aware of this and even though they did not want to seem so forward or give me a rushed impression, they impressed upon me the need to plan quickly in order to increase my chances of surviving cancer.

---

2   Metastitic - 1.The process by which cancer spreads from the place at which it first arose as a primary tumor to distant locations in the body. 2. The cancer resulting from the spread of the primary tumor... For example, "**metastatic** melanoma" refers to melanoma that has spread beyond the skin to distant organs.

You'd think that this information about the severe implications of not reaching a decision early enough would've caused me to rouse myself from the stupor that seemed to have enveloped my thinking, rational brain. NO, I was too sucked into the despair of not living to see fifty at the very least. It was on one of such brooding occasions that a close male friend of mine found me and took some rather unconventional measures to set me straight. (14 yrs later at the time of print, I am so grateful for these action steps literally)

My friend Vito found me sobbing almost uncontrollably and asked me to stand up. I wasn't in the mood to be engaged in any antics and so I asked him, rather brashly why I should stand up. He ignored my brashness and instead, pulled me up so that we stood an arm's length apart. He asked me to investigate the square patch in the carpet on the floor where I was standing and as I lowered my head to look, he pushed me backwards. It wasn't a gentle push and I did not have a gentle reaction either; even though I was suddenly knocked off balance, I came back swinging with a right hook.

I really wanted to hit him for pushing me like that and I was well on the way to doing so. The calm looks on his face unsettled me even further. I was peeved and he was calm! How on earth was this supposed to be his reaction in the face of my anger? I know I'd have a different look on my face if I had suddenly pushed someone completely off-balance and the person was looking to get back at me. At this point, I also noticed that I had no tears in my eyes anymore; where had they suddenly fled to? However now anger rose!

He responded calmly to my initial question as to why he had pushed me in that manner. He told me to look at the square again and see how much it had consumed me completely. I took another look and while a part of my defence antenna was still on high alert and probably anticipating another sudden jolt, I quickly saw what message my friend was trying to pass across to me.

Gasp; this shifted my perspective on my situation, as I was consumed.

In my annoyance, I had failed to notice that I had moved from the square I was initially standing in and this was as a result of the force of the push. It dawned on me that I had been figuratively standing in a similar square of my own with my reaction to my diagnosis. The feeling of getting annoyed at being pushed out of that square by the words from the doctors and the people around me urging me to decide fast. This didn't sit well initially. Deciding fast had to be the right decision and making that decision didn't come without some conflict and internal stress.

I was channelling the rage in the wrong direction; inwards and towards the people whose words, when heeded, were

supposed to make the path easier for me. As such, try as I might to rouse myself from that square patch; I wasn't making any headway because I was shutting everyone who could help me out.

This realisation came with a bucket load of tears, I was in overwhelm of emotions inside and out. I had a feeling I had been saved by this push, hard and all as it was. The feeling of that push still lingers within me today, not to get sucked into the vortex of negativity again.

Profound yet TRUE!

I thanked my friend for the help he had lent me in this rather unconventional manner and resolved to reach a decision right away no matter what the emotional or psychological cost maybe. I knew how to draw and read map contours and with my background in sewing, I thought I might able to get a more defined view of what is at stake with each procedure. I settled down and drew my breast to scale so I could understand the right way to go about my procedure.

Beyond this method, I had tried earlier to find out from women who had survived breast cancer similar to my own condition how they had reached their own decision and spoke to members of the Queensland Cancer Council who offered more scientific explanations that I found very helpful for my decision-making process.

It had taken me about three weeks to get to the point where I had that insightful encounter with my friend, but soon after, I arrived at the required conclusion as to how I would like to proceed and the major propelling factor for me was this encounter with my friend.

Drawing my breast to scale, was a very logical and straight forward step for me. I could see that there wouldn't be much of the breast left if I chose to go through with a lumpectomy. From what I gathered from the Council discussion; the chances of a secondary breast cancer occurrence were greater if the breast where first lumps had appeared were still in place. Also, the chance that my lymph glands may already be infected also made the idea of getting a lumpectomy a very impractical one. So, in the light of understanding all these factors that were in play in my unique situation, I chose to follow through with a full mastectomy.

This decision all happened over the weekend with only days before I had to break the news to the surgeon assigned to my case. He seemed startled that I had decided to go with a full mastectomy, and I showed him the drawing I had made and how there wouldn't be much left of my right breast if I decided to have a lumpectomy. There was also the fact that the actual size of the lumps was still mostly unknown and would only be known when I'm undergoing the surgical procedure. The mastectomy

was scheduled for the 8th of May, 2006 and by this time, the lump that was in stage four had already started to invert my nipple. It was a full mastectomy and in the process of the procedure, it was found that one out of my nine lymph glands had been infected, although the infection had not spread into the bloodstream. Once the surgeon witnessed the evidence, I had undertaken with making this decision, he replied to me he wished all his patience had the ability to get clarity as I had. He also shared it would be an honour to operate on your breast as he could see I was totally at a place of acceptance. Huge steps huge awareness and huge sigh of relief. The next phase was about to begin.

Chemotherapy followed immediately after the mastectomy, like around 6 weeks later. I had my sutures taken out and met with the oncologist. The schedule for my treatment was six months with three weeks intervals for two specific types of chemotherapy. The first two weeks of chemotherapy really impacted me hard. I was a complete emotional wreck and even more so when losing my hair started with impact. I struggled to come to terms with living for some time without my hair.

Many people lose their hair when on this journey, however for me it wasn't a good thing internally. I was in shock with the vanity of the experience on top of the breast loss.

It never really felt the same wearing the wig that most women opt to wear. Losing the parts of me that I would usually never believe could be lost took a toll on my psychological state. I struggled with the options of dark colours to wear. I was a blonde and a dark hair wig just did not do anything for me let alone my confidence. I finally found a blonde short hair wig and gained my confidence once I got used to it.

I'd wake up on some mornings still wondering how come this was happening to me and I'd be miserable for quite some time. Waking up after the first batch of the second lot of chemotherapy that I had to undergo to no feeling in my feet isolated me even further from the outside world. I couldn't drive to any place and frankly, just having a very heavy feelings in my legs was terrifying.

The second lot of chemotherapy was recommended for me to ensure that there would be no cancerous cells left that could instigate a secondary breast cancer, which according to my doctors, may not be as lenient as the first one. They called this second lot a white chemo session while the first one was called red chemo.

The mode of application for the two sessions differed in some ways. The first lot, the red chemo, was called the fire engine and this was my body's first encounter with the chemicals that would help obliterate the cancerous cells that my body harboured. The name is very fitting, I must say, and I had four batches of this chemotherapy administered directly into my body via a slow drip injection into my left arm. The second lot of chemo, the white chemo, was somewhat different in the way it was administered. It wasn't administered directly into my body like the first lot, however through a [3]Port-a-cath placed in my veins which transported the fluids gradually to my heart; one dose taking about six to eight hours to be administered properly. I sat in the large comfy style chairs for close to six hours waiting for the fluids to drip into my bloodstream and be transported to my heart before I could begin to move around. These were all treatments I received as an out-patient which meant I still had to find my way home after the drugs had been administered.

My family was far away and although I had a sister who came around often to help me around the house as the chemotherapy kicked in full-time, it was still a great deal of effort for me to just keep my house habitable. I'd never been one to be really tired out even after work and when I found myself falling asleep on the train on my way home, I usually put it down to having an early morning or going to bed late the night before.

---

3   Port-a-cath is attached to a **catheter** (a thin, flexible tube) that is threaded into a large vein above the right side of the heart called the superior vena cava. A **port-a-cath** is **used to** give intravenous fluids, blood transfusions, chemotherapy, and other drugs. It is also **used for** taking blood samples.

During my chemotherapy, especially after the white one, I was constantly fatigued, and I could barely move around. I could barely do the dishes without feeling like I had run a three-hour marathon. It was like I had lost the zest for engaging in anything at all and my body was simply a reflection of my thoughts. I had a couple of friends visit me occasionally and a couple of aunts and uncles called in for a cuppa. I was glad of it because when they were there, it took my mind off the pain and despair. On bad days however, it wouldn't make so much of a difference because I'd still feel isolated from them in the sense that it was my body that cancer inhabited and no matter how many words they tried to say to soothe my pain or despair, I still found room to be bitter and alone in my emotional pain.

Luckily for me, those bad days were far between because as I got to know later on from engaging in therapy sessions, the mindset is a very important factor that lends to how much easier we are able to handle suffering and tragedy that comes around.

Hints and Tips

- Be thankful for any help and or assistance; you can let your pride go when illness strikes.
- People offer help because they care;

LET ME GET THIS OFF MY CHEST
- COPING WITH BREAST CANCER ALONE *by* JANICE MUIR

Chapter Seven

Doubt is the key to knowledge.

– Iranian Proverb

Self Sufficient

Financially, I was in some trouble. Alongside my feelings of being alone and having to face the full course of treatments by myself, I was really worried about my finances and try as I might to not let this make my condition escalate, it remained a nudging fear in a part of my mind.

As I was living in a single unit house that did not require a great deal of finances to maintain, I was thankful to have that roof over my head at the very least. Upon leaving the hospital immediately after my diagnosis, I called the office to inform them I wouldn't be back until the next day and as I made this call, I couldn't help but wonder how much longer I'd be able to keep the job before I couldn't work anymore.

I had been worried about securing a permanent job before the diagnosis and so, you can imagine how much more worried I became when it was evident that even the temporary work that I had which was aiding my survival at the time wasn't something I could continue for much longer. I was really wiped out. I was really in dire straits with my finances and this bothered me a great deal as I left the hospital. There would be huge costs for the duration of my treatments, and I couldn't be sure that my insurance could cover these costs completely. I had to find a way to make things work.

Thankfully, a decision I had made earlier when I was upgrading my car in Brisbane served me well around this time. While getting the upgrade, I was encouraged to take out an insurance package that could cover the costs if I had an accident happen with the car or in the event that I was suddenly unable to make the payments for the car loan as usual due to a tragic event or terminal illness. This second clause would prevent my car from being repossessed when I become unable to pay the car loans and so, the insurance would cover my car payments until I was able to foot the bills once more.

At the time, it did not cross my mind how much this choice could aid my life, yet I decided to go with it because it wasn't such a bad idea to have that kind of insurance

because you can never tell what's around the next corner of life. Little did I know that it would prove to be an indispensable decision for me. Around this time too, I had adopted some refinancing options with the Bank of Queensland because I felt I needed to get some degree of control of my funds so I could better understand what I'll need to get ahead and edge myself closer to financial stability.

Those two decisions saved me from completely going under with the stress of finding the finances for completing my treatment and with the fact that my car would not be repossessed, I could also get around easily. Being an out-patient at the hospital wasn't such a bad situation because as long as I could drive, I was able to get to the hospital and back without hassle.

I could not have foreseen the events that subsequently took place in my life as I moved to Brisbane and made these choices about my finances, but at my most trying periods, I was thankful that I had made some wise decisions at that point.

Hints and Tips

- ❦ Your intuition is guiding you all the time;
- ❦ Listen Act and be Grateful;
- ❦ Say 'thank you' often!

Chapter Eight

The greatest revelation is stillness.

– Laozi

Chemo Numbness Effect

Waking up to numbed feet was the weirdest sensation I felt during my treatments, but this was nothing as weird as the sensation I felt when I had my first shower after the full mastectomy. The nurse had warned me that this might happen, however I was not even remotely prepared for the reality.

As the water gushed out of the shower head as it always had for the past five years I'd lived in the house, it was eerie for me that on this particular day, it was only beating down on one breast because that was all I now had. It brought more of my situation home to me in as glaring a manner as possible; I had just lost a breast to cancer.

Chemotherapy may have isolated me from my environment a great deal however, the real isolating factor soon became the fact that I had lost my breast and coupled with that, my hair had grown weak from radiation and fell off at every chance.

The impact of this reality on my personal image was profound. I usually prided my looks on well-rounded, full-body shape and somehow, with one of my breasts gone, it seemed to me like I was now potentially disfigured. I battled a diminished self-image for the longest time and even now, I'm still a bit self-conscious even though I wear a prosthetic one.

There's always a feeling niggling in some part of my brain which often wonders if people can see right away that I have a prosthetic breast and not a real one and if it makes them look at me as a lesser person. The apprehension from having to always think about this was heavier around the time I had just completed the mastectomy. Every shower I had after that still had me shocked at the reality, but it slowly waned as I grew accustomed to being that way.

It caused some tension in my social life and I constantly fretted over my appearance, yet even this too became a less and less concern as it became more evident to me that I should be more grateful for having the means to put this ailment behind me and get a chance to move on with my life albeit without my right breast.

Physically, I was not in the best of shapes. After the second lot of chemotherapy, I woke up to very numb feet as I tried to stand up from the bed in the morning. I literally fell to the floor. I thought nobody prepared me for this adverse effect. The chemicals that I'd been pumped with the day before had me a little concerned and I decided someone needed to explain to me what had happened. It remained that way after six hours and then I called the hospital to report the observation because it was beginning to worry me greatly. The staff nor the doctor when he rang could not understand the impact why my feet were numb. It was bad enough with the heavy feeling in my legs let alone numb feet.

I couldn't get around the house and get some items I wanted or get any chores done. I was without any explanation from the hospital. I proceeded to see a health practitioner and it was here that I witnessed so much change in my blood and how it was coping with some blood analysis. I was only then able to understand the heavy feeling in the legs. This numbness in my feet remained constant throughout the three months of the white chemotherapy. I had to bear the discomfort of walking around with no feeling in my feet.

These periods were unsettling for me because here again, I was facing a reality that I would never have thought possible in my wildest imaginations. Being able to walk around, stand or run with two legs is a huge blessing and it took my experience of numbness for the whole of three months to drill this realization into my head and I cannot completely describe how many more areas in my life that I had previously taken for granted that were really important for the overall functioning of my body and its effect on my daily activities.

Despite the reports and stories of pain that is associated with receiving chemotherapy and the medications that are usually prescribed for the pain, I experienced a lot less physical pain than most of the accounts I'd heard or read about. My pain was mostly of an emotional or psychological kind.

Thankfully, the doctors prescribed anti-nausea medication after I made it clear to them that I was going through this whole process alone and as such I could not afford to have periods where I'd suddenly feel the need to vomit or have to run to the toilet because there'd be no one available to clean it up and also seeing as I already had my hands full with the big C. These anti-nausea drugs did have a huge side effect they caused me to develop a huge appetite, however, and by the time my treatments were over, my weight was a significant amount so much so that I looked really huge in my own eyes. Another part of my self-confidence emerged

The impact without any anti-nausea drugs would have been huge to manage on my own however I was to experience a huge amount of feeling lethargic and sometimes spent a good part of the day in bed. No energy at all.

I could not muster the energy most of the time during my chemotherapy treatment to complete even the simplest tasks. My body might protest this trade-off however I had to work with the three weeks process. Week one was allow myself to feel what I felt and get by with the basics of everything. TV became my companion. I didn't eat anywhere near the food in week one as in week three.

Week two I could muster a small amount of effort to walk a bit more, getting to and from the toilet at times was an effort. However, I did feel some spark here and there to want to do something more, I know I wrote a lot of long story like emails to friends. It was my release and communication with the world as well. I did use the phone many times to contact friends and family. Thank goodness for this device.

The third week was freedom week, I felt so much better in myself I could go for a walk and I could drive a car for short distances. Thank goodness I had an automatic car made it a lot easier. I'd do what housework I could and start to prepare meals for the next three weeks as this was the only week, I had the strength. The other downside was the third week I ate more so, I had a significant weight gain. The side effect of the chemo was I ate a lot more biscuits as my comfort food. This weight gain of 25 kg turned out to only be a small delay on the purple patch I was going through at the time. I did lose it all back to my normal self after the treatment was finished.

Hints and Tips

- ❧ When faced with adversity we must stop and listen to our inner voice and be guided accordingly.;
- ❧ Meditation allows us to still the mind.
- ❧ Stillness allows us to see the better outcomes.

LET ME GET THIS OFF MY CHEST
- COPING WITH BREAST CANCER ALONE *by* JANICE MUIR

Chapter Nine

Only in the darkness can you see the stars.

– Martin Luther King Jr.

Finding Hope and Healing

The journey for anyone diagnosed with breast cancer (or any cancer at all for that matter) is never a smooth one. The stories I was privileged to hear from many cancer survivors were really heart-wrenching to say the very least. Many questions surfaced in my mind as I deliberated these stories however one question that always surfaced in my mind when I heard each person's story was how they went about surviving this ordeal because from where I was standing, it was one huge hurdle. What was it that kept them going throughout the treatments and even after they were cleared of cancer? How could they live with any positivity in the face of the chance of recurrence?

I was going to find out though I would not categorize my journey as the exact same with the other women's whose stories shook me, therefore it was a life-changing experience regardless. I didn't think I would lose a breast ever. It was part of my body. How could an illness make me lose something that was mine? Not possible; at least not while I still had it intact. I didn't even realise how the cancer started until I was diagnosed – it was a hard lesson to learn after the fact, yet it is something many of us do.

The people that I spoke to while trying to reach a decision on which procedure to take told me that I would find a way to cope. Although I couldn't see how I could find a way from where I was standing or sitting. I knew deep down that I had to find a way, if I really said I wanted to hit fifty and be alive to see my grandchildren and perhaps tie the knot with a handsome, attractive man of my own someday.

After hearing the news of my diagnosis and wanting to get the whole process over with as fast as I could, which was not happening fast for me. At the time I often wondered can't we do all of this at once. Nah! it was one step at a time. Starting on the path to getting it over with were two different things as you have seen from the length of time it took me to even arrive at my choice of surgical procedure. I felt so much better in myself once this decision was made. This was the same thing for me with wanting to remain strong and resilient for my fight against cancer and being strong and resilient.

Something that I drew on from inside of me, that I did not understand, let alone know about beforehand.

I figured after a couple of months into my treatment that it wasn't really a single period or moment in my journey that constituted my strength or resilience. It was a compendium of every moment I was able to wake and make an effort at living despite the cancer that had inhabited my system, threatening to end my life.

My journey with cancer and the inner strength it revealed that was latent in me, really altered my entire outlook towards life. I was alive until, my cancer diagnosis yet to what degree, I could not rightly say; not until the cancer put things into perspective for me. It was very tempting to guilt-trip myself into feeling that I could've been better at taking care of my body so that I would not have to be diagnosed at all. I quickly dropped this mindset because it wasn't practical for my healing process.

In order to show up for every round or batch of chemotherapy, I had to keep up my positivity levels and this was no mean feat. Living with the knowledge that the steps that you are taking to rid yourself of an illness may not really pan out eventually is not very inspiring. There was a risk it may not be successful – or we won't go there!

Understanding that you need to carry on with these steps regardless of this knowledge is something that one could even define as cruelty. Even in one's most helpless moments, there are no insights that can tell you for certain that if you take this course of treatment for a certain amount of time, you will be free of this illness.

The positivity must come from somewhere and I quickly learned that it wasn't going to be a fixed store of positivity. There wasn't going to be a space in my head reserved simply for motivation and inspiration. It would have to be a continuous and conscious effort to stay that way because the events that transpire will inevitably deplete the stores of positivity and require replenishing.

At times purely exhausting, yet I kept going with doing my best to inspire my day every day, one day at a time was my motto.

Getting to the hospital on the first day for the commencement of my chemotherapy, I found that they had not prepared for my arrival to start the treatment and this was a huge emotional setback for me. I know the amount of adrenaline that I had pumped up just to get myself through the doors of the hospital for the treatments and it really seemed like a callous move on the part of all the staff involved at the hospital. I had prepared to begin treatment on that day and so, my body was on co-operate mode with directions from my brain and all I met was this incompetence on the hospital's part. I just really lost a lot of my nerve at that point.

I was broken to some degree, and the nurses witnessed this. Losing the breast one minute then pouring of chemicals into the body the next step. As I write today, I can sense that feeling of mixed anticipation of how I would cope mentally let alone physically from having a chemical enter my body – the no show of treatment starting on that day rocked me with agitation. Had I made the right decision?

Things seemed to be getting to far ahead for me. I was sure that the factors that conspire to turn things around for the better were that someone was not paying attention and I wasn't going to get through any of this alive. Not the best thought pattern to have, however I was in the chair and nothing was going to happen. Well not this day anyway.

After I had calmed down and the nurses were rechecking why my chemo was missed. (No explanation someone goofed the orders). Trust me the nurses were not expecting my outburst of emotions. I was visibly distraught. On leaving the hospital knowing I was back the next day to do it all over again was not a pleasant experience to have to face.

With my emotions now calmed down after a great deal of effort I arrived back at the hospital for the first round on the next day. Once I was in the checking in point, I was assured by several nurses that the treatment was now ready for me. All previous matters were set right at the hospital. I began to get to know the nurses as I noticed they all checked up on me as the treatment began. It was at this period I knew I was going to be okay.

Shortly after this time, my daughter had to return to Darwin after having spent six weeks with me after my diagnosis and through my mastectomy.

My daughter had shared her time and had been a great support during this difficult period and for that I am eternally grateful. I was also very aware that at some point she would have to return despite it being a difficult time of departure. I had to come to terms the road ahead would be achieved in some way shape and form. I couldn't see too far into the future other than making it though chemotherapy.

The first night of chemotherapy was a nightmare; nothing was working for me.

I felt so loaded with chemicals and all the thoughts in my mind were about how I was being pumped with these chemicals that could potentially destroy the healthy cells in my body as well as destroy the harmful, cancerous ones. I might've started to even envisage things going wrong and the chemotherapy being the problem even though they might've just been figments of my imagination;

these chemicals were just too alien for me. I alternated frequently between lying in bed and on the couch, trying to find the most comfortable places to rest and the most convenient place to be so that I did not have to move around so often and increase my fatigue.

As part of my treatments, I found out in a small research I conducted that supplements could aid my recuperation from the effects of the chemotherapy however, the oncologist advised that these supplements would not have so much of an impact on the process and so it would be a waste of my time and resources. My nutritionist and I, however, researched the information that the hospital had provided about my chemo treatments and found the kind of supplements that could help me cope with the two lots of chemotherapy sessions.

I knew at this point I was back on the road to recovery yet a long and winding road as well.

I figured that since the doctors did not flag the supplements as impeding the work of the chemicals used for the chemotherapy, I could try them and see if they'd work or relieve the initial pain and discolouration even a little bit. I needed all the help I could get with coping with the chemotherapy and I was open to trying more techniques and methods beyond the traditionally accepted ones practised in the hospitals.

Having an open-minded approach is how I stumbled across alternative medicine (long before I was diagnosed) this too aided my coping with chemotherapy and radiation.

What did eventuate for me was I was referred to a very intelligent nutritionist and he understood the workings of chemo. What happened was at my appointments with the nutritionist he looked at my bloods and with his knowledge and research done around my chemo, he was able to work with the components that worked synergistically with my body to counter balance and help the healing on the inside. I used very reputable products that agreed with where my body was at and this helped me to stay as well as I could on this chemo journey.

Hints and Tips

- Sometimes we must look outside the medical arena to find what our body needs;
- Your intuition will guide you;
- Just Allow and Take the ACTION.

LET ME GET THIS OFF MY CHEST
- COPING WITH BREAST CANCER ALONE *by* JANICE MUIR

Chapter Ten

*Take every chance you get in life,
because somethings only happen once!*

– *Karen Gibbs*

Mindset Awareness

Earlier on in the book, you might've seen the point I highlighted the effect of one's mind on the way their body reacts to the circumstances that befall it. This knowledge is the type that most people know however, they relegate it to a remote part of their consciousness as they get swept up in daily cares and struggles for survival.

As a "healthy" person, I was one of those people that had this mindset. I never really gave much thought to the idea that my mindset could greatly influence what happens to me. I was more focused on what I could see physically and added to the stressful nature of the jobs that I usually engaged in; my mindset was usually the last thing on the list of things I need to take note of in order to get through each day. Sure, there are infrequent spots in between where I'd try to keep up a habit of positive self-talk on tough days at work, or during the period I was providing support for my partner as he battled Alzheimer's. These periods did not last so long.

Getting diagnosed with cancer slowed me down a great deal and caused me to really start paying attention to these overlooked areas in my life. It brought many flaws that were in my lifestyle to the forefront. Even though I might've chosen to have these flaws broken down or revealed to me in a gentler way, I cannot say that any other method would've had as profound an effect as the fact that my very life hung in the balance if I did not internalize these lessons. I was forced to admit my impractical work and lifestyle choices as well as my dieting and if I wasn't open-minded about these things, I would most likely never have made as quick a recovery as I did once my treatments ended.

An essential part in effecting the change in mindset that was necessary for the alternative medicine techniques I adopted required that I accept responsibility for the way I had structured my life; work, diet, health, etc. as well as forgive my negligence in the past. This combination would serve as a strong basis for the improvements that I longed to implement in my life and would increase my ability to stay committed to this path even after my cancer journey has become a thing of the past.

These techniques which included Reiki, meditation, counselling, chiropractic therapy, etc., were focused on harnessing energy fields and healing techniques beyond the ones primarily used by the traditional medical practitioners in a bid to alleviate pain and facilitate recovery. These techniques are not completely backed by science due solely to the lack of quantifiable and empirical proof that they are effective in curing ailments.

The positive reports from cancer survivors, however, were not something I could look past and I am glad that I did not look past these techniques to rely solely on the medical sciences because they greatly improved my situation and invariably impacted my well-being. If for nothing else, these alternative medicine practices helped me calm myself and slow down to allow my body to heal itself well from all the effects of my negligence.

A standard Reiki technique involves the use of the palms to heal. This palm-healing technique was made popular in Japan and involves the transfer of a universal healing energy from the palms of the practitioner onto the patient or recipient of the therapy. This therapy was effective in greatly reducing the emotional pain that often burdened me during the period I battled breast cancer.

The energy that is harnessed by the practitioners and masters of this art of healing focuses on the areas in the body where energy has stagnated and these kinds of stagnant energy blocks can be found in people with physical injury or people going through emotional pain. This healing technique aims at releasing these energy blocks in a manner, not unlike acupuncture, that aids relaxation, reduces pain and increases both emotional and physical healing.

Reiki is a technique that has been met with much dubious reports and claims that its efficacy is mere speculation. For a time, I was sceptical about adopting it and this was only until I conducted my own research and discovered that the efficacy of the entire process does not rest solely on the expertise or professionalism of the practitioner, however also on the recipient of the therapy. I figured that the origin of these doubts about the technique stemmed from an inadequate understanding of the overall process and all the factors that ensure the success of every session.

The technique for chiropractic therapy is a little more hands-on than the Reiki technique and it is mostly centred around manipulating the spine in such a way as to improve overall physical function of the body. It is a very popular technique adopted by most women undergoing chemotherapy or radiation for the treatment of breast cancer. The relationship that has been observed between the body's structure and its ability to function is the major foundation for the practice of chiropractic and so, it follows that as long as the structure of the body (mostly the spine) is in its normal position, the body is completely capable of healing itself in the event of an injury or illness.

The routine for this technique is usually more advanced and it may not be suitable for everyone who indicates an interest in obtaining the treatment. For me, it was a huge relief finding out that I could receive the treatment although this came around the time that I had already regained most of my strength after the first lot of the six-month-long red chemotherapy. Four treatments of Red chemo and four treatments of white six months in total.

The therapy provided relief for the back and joint pains that I experienced as a result of the treatments I received for the breast cancer as well as the occasional headaches that came during the first few months of chemotherapy. It was combined with massages to achieve the most lasting effect as well as to lower the discomfort that I felt from the force applied to the various joints in my body during the adjustments. The chiropractor on my case had to take extra care with me because of the surgery I had undergone and this did not pose so much of a problem for me because I was gladder to have this kind of therapy at my disposal during those tough days.

For many survivors of breast cancer and women still battling it, there are reports of further diagnosis with clinical depression as a result of the psychological and physical pain and other implications of the disease. This might've been the case for me if I wasn't so wrapped up in trying my best to stay strong in order to get through the many processes that were required for me to enter the clear zone. Since that fateful Wednesday, the only thoughts that filled my mind was the best way to tackle everything that my condition would require of me and so, the subsequent days and months were spent focusing my energies on being strong.

The result of this is that I only knew pain when I wasn't trying to be strong and this would usually be early in the mornings as I woke up and tried to get out of bed or get up from the couch. These were the moments when my guards weren't shielding me completely from the effects of my situation; those moments before you start to speak the day's positivity into your being and slowly regain the

resolve to get through the day. These were the moments that pain could seep into my consciousness and I'd be tempted to sink into an unwholesome frame of mind.

It wasn't always so easy for me to rouse myself to pursue those positive thought patterns because often, the negativity and doubts would resurface with renewed strength that I would give into them for some time. These emotions that conflicted inside me continued for the most part of my cancer journey and most of the time, I found it difficult to open to my family, even my daughter.

With her, I felt as though I should spare her the spectacle of my suffering and so, each chance I got, I tried to express positivity so that she wouldn't have to worry so much nor be aware of the exact degree of my emotional turmoil. A lot of people disagreed with my stance on opening to my daughter. It also caused some tension between us however I know that I did not need her to suffer all over again after losing her father to Alzheimer's and truth be told, the process of needing to stay and appear strong and positive for my daughter actually aided my overall resilience and that's how I know that I was on the right track with my decision.

Opening all the emotional baggage that was in me was so much easier with the counsellors at the Queensland Cancer Council. I had a great consultant assigned to me and I was able to constantly speak up about the emotional pressures I felt and without the fear of being judged. This ability to open greatly helped my process especially as I also started up on my alternative medicine techniques and with everything falling into place with my treatments, my apprehension started abating.

I started to feel much more hopeful that I could indeed fight this battle and win. There was a snag along the way, however, when I was told that I needed to take a second lot of chemotherapy so that they could be sure that all the cancer cells had been destroyed no matter the area they were located in. Even though this was only a precaution and for good reason, I could not help but feel a short burst of dread at the possibility of a recurrence and how I may just cave in if that does happen sometime in the future.

I wedged this doubt out of my mind immediately it surfaced and stiffened my spine and hoped for the best. This was a great stance for me to take and it was not long before I started regaining my strength and colour began returning to my looks as soon as the second lot was over.

Hints and Tips

- The journey begins with one small step regardless of it being an accident and or an illness or whatever the case may be, it's in taking the first small step.

- You are guided with each step, the naysayers will give you advice and it's up to you if you follow or not, your intuition will agree or disagree.

- Never look at how high the ladder is on this journey always know it won't last forever; two rungs today fall back 3 tomorrow and be informed to take another step forward the next day.

- Never ever give up!

LET ME GET THIS OFF MY CHEST
- COPING WITH BREAST CANCER ALONE *by* JANICE MUIR

Chapter Eleven

In the long run, we shape our lives and we shape ourselves. The process never ends until we die, and the choices we make are ultimately our own responsibility.

– Eleanor Roosevelt

Five Years Later – All Clear

My cancer journey was an eye-opener for me. Coming face-to-face with my mortality really turned my priorities around and the lifestyle changes that ensued are what I would describe as imperative for any woman to adopt as they grow older.

I never really gave much thought to coming down with a terminal illness until I was diagnosed and so, I was not really the most health-conscious woman on the planet. The force with which every part of this disease hit me is one that is deeply ingrained in my subconscious. At the time I was providing care and support to my partner when he was diagnosed with Alzheimer's, I thought that I couldn't feel as stressed or as emotionally distraught as I felt at that time, however with breast cancer, the experience and its effect on my emotional and psychological state was on a completely different level.

Nothing could have prepared me for what I was to witness.

You can imagine how clear the wrong choices I had made at any point in my work or diet plans were as I struggled with cancer. It was expressed in HD format and there was no getting around the reality. If I had been telling myself a story about how I never really had time to settle down enough to get a balanced meal into my system because I was always so busy. I know now that these were a load of impractical excuses that would never serve me well and should never have featured in my subconscious at all.

Most of the stories that I heard from different people who had survived cancer after I was newly diagnosed usually highlighted the fact that they were thankful for the experience. As time went on, I learned it was because of the new perspective and outlook in life that it afforded them.

I have a slightly different opinion however and it is that whilst in the pain from the following months that ensued, I remember mostly thinking a situation where one didn't need to go through this much just to learn new and healthier perspectives would be a lot better. This was how the need started burning in me to share my experience in such a way as to encourage people to improve their standard and lifestyle, even though they are not living with cancer or don't have it expressed to some degree in their genes.

In my opinion, changes don't have to be made only after surviving a terminal illness or some other tragic event in one's life. I remember continually wishing, as I learned the important yet mostly unknown things about my body, that I had known all of this before the diagnosis. It didn't really matter at that point and since then, I have slowly come to terms with the fact that things would happen in life without warning. No matter how much you believe that you might've been better placed if you had taken precautions. This realization is only a result of hindsight bias and so, the lesson has been learned certainly. As you move forward, there are more events that can potentially floor you still.

This mindset really empowered me to recognize the unique and singular experience that is my life. As I worked on an outline for this book, I had to struggle with the parts to put in and how in-depth it had to be in order to make any reader relate to my story. It was as I accepted the fact that all I only had to really worry about was representing my journey in the way that it really happened, that writing this book became so much easier for me.

This journey with breast cancer that I had to undertake was an individual one, despite the presence of so many other contributors. I do not know why I would need to swap my experiences with someone else because deep down, all I kept thinking was how well-suited my experiences were to impact me the most and even unleash the latent strengths in me. I felt a new, strong disposition towards achieving everything that I wanted and this time around, I had a very clear priority and that was to focus on being the best person I could be for myself and for the people around me. I had survived a gruelling ordeal and battle with a deadly disease and in my opinion, every other event or thing that seemed to have been an obstacle to my achievements of all the other hopes and aspirations I had paled in comparison and so, it was a new burst of life for me.

In 2011, the results came back, and the cancer found in my right breast was gone! I was set to take on life with a zeal like none I'd ever applied before. I started with aspects in my life that just did not fit my newly minted standard of living anymore.

At the time of writing this book and a recent breast screen check, still clear of cancer 15+ yrs on!! Hooray.

LET ME GET THIS OFF MY CHEST
- COPING WITH BREAST CANCER ALONE *by*   JANICE MUIR

Hints and Tips

- Follow what your heart shares to you;
- Nobody knows your journey until they are there themselves;
- Be kind to self and share gifts to you, Because You are special;
- Look at what you eat be mindful of alkaline and acidic bodies;
- Keep on keeping on... cause;
- You can do this!

LET ME GET THIS OFF MY CHEST
- COPING WITH BREAST CANCER ALONE *by* JANICE MUIR

Chapter Twelve

We have no problems only situations. Not all problems have solutions, and all situations have outcomes.

– John Edward Gray

Seven Outcomes

I have always had a bucket list of items I wanted to do as I got older however after my cancer journey, those items took a back seat in the light of new items that took precedence on the list. I compiled these new items into bullet points that I'd love to share with you.

1. **Take care of your body:**

    This is number one on the list for very valid reasons. It is simply the most important factor in living the fullest life that you can. This was my number one item because the way I saw it, anything can happen to that body and frankly, you may be helpless to prevent it when you have a greater disposition to that random happening such as having the BRCA gene in your bloodline however, the least you can do is make it really difficult for those genes and other environmental factors to express themselves.

    I found out while taking supplements alongside my chemotherapy that the impact of everything that is put into our bodies is truly profound. I understood the need to balance the alkaline and acidic food intake in my body in order to keep my body functions at their most optimum.

    Lowering stress as often as possible was a goal that featured high on my list of taking care of my body. It did not make sense to me that I should work on eating right while still stressing my body out; it would simply become a wasted effort in my opinion.

2. *Material assets matter, yet not so much:*

I'm a stickler for financial stability and while moving to Brisbane, in 2001 it was top on my list yet, after facing cancer, my priorities shifted a little bit. I still understand that finances are an important aspect of my life and the life of everyone else really and the way to go about taking care of the finances had to change. In the kinds of jobs that I'd been engaged with prior to my encounter with cancer, it was easy to become swept up in a gale of "busy-ness" that could potentially reduce your lifespan by a great amount. This would all be because you are trying to make ends meet or you're just climbing the rungs on the ladder of success or achievements in any field that you have chosen.

As slow as I became during my cancer treatment, this slowing down afforded me the space to really think about the path I had taken thus far to gain financial stability and to evaluate its overall impact in other areas of my life which were just as important. It did not make sense to me that I would sacrifice the preciousness of good health for any kind of material success and it only made sense to really work at pacing oneself in order to take every event that comes along in my stride. It was important that I had some financial options to help my procurement of good health care yet, in the same vein, it would be important going forward to account for the other parts of my life that were important too alongside financial stability.

3. *Understand your family history extensively:*

At forty-seven, I was sure I still had many more productive years. Matter of fact, I was banking on it with the way my life was structured and with the hopes that I had moved to Brisbane with. I was one of the many women who are mostly unaware and possibly unaware of the prevalence of the BRCA gene in the family bloodline and the full extent of that prevalence.

I'd been told about this prevalence when I was twelve or thirteen years of age and suffice it to say that the eventuality wasn't a thought I entertained for an extended period. I also applied one common flaw in my thinking and understanding of the prevalence of the gene and this was by believing that if I was ever going to be diagnosed with breast cancer, it'll be much later in my life, possibly around my sixties and seventies.

How wrong my thinking would be!

This was not an educated conclusion and the result is that if there was a chance that some lifestyle choice or diet plan that could delay or even inhibit the expression of the gene at any point in my adult life, I completely missed out on that solution because of the belief that I already held. After my diagnosis, as I read about more cases.

I even came across many breast cancers cases in women so much younger than myself and I saw even more clearly the impracticality of my belief. Thoughts that featured frequently in my mind as I received treatments, no matter how often I tried to stop myself from indulging them, included deep regret for not gaining a better knowledge of my body as a whole and my family's health history.

4. *If you're in the "C" woods, inform yourself about your diagnosis:*

It was tempting to quickly cover up any curiosity or questions that quickly arose when the specialist first told me that I had three lumps that were malignant. It would've really helped me if there was a magical way to get the specialist to "un-say" what he had said about the lumps in my breast, just so my life would not fall apart. Truth is, once the reality set in, the best thing I could do for myself was to inform myself.

As I said before, anyway I could aid the people around me to provide the best kind of care and support for my ailment, I was willing to try and that's exactly what I did with canvassing for information. It was through my research in my bid to inform myself that I discovered the right supplements and alternative medicine; factors that greatly influenced my ability to bounce back as soon as my treatments were over.

Starting from my understanding of the importance of going through with the right procedure (a full mastectomy) to the best practices to adopt for a changed lifestyle afterwards, information was an important part of my journey.

Instead of the distress, it is often thought to bring to anyone who actively seeks it when they're terminally ill, it helped me remain calm as I believed that I knew the role each step, medication, healing technique or practice that I took would be playing in my healing process.

Getting to know about the prevalence of the BRCA gene that runs in my family as well as the presence of elevated oestrogen levels in my own system allowed me the space to understand that these elements played a role in my diagnosis. They would continue to play a role in my system even after my cancer journey and this helped me take steps to monitor my system better to reduce chances of recurrence even more.

5. *You're stronger than you know; give yourself a chance:*

In the darkest period in my adulthood, I stumbled upon a resilience that I did not know that I possessed, and I have become a different person ever since. I was sure that I couldn't cope and in dark moments such as the one that my friend found me in before I decided on a full mastectomy, the only thing that occupied my mind was the fact that I was going to die after all.

It took me a while to choose to fight and I was glad that I made that choice because the other side of the struggle is a truly wonderful place to be. As I mentioned earlier, I believe now that tragic events do not have to take place before you can adopt the best practices for your lifestyle, yet it goes further than that.

Our lives are a unique blend of experiences that conspire to shape our different realities and the way I see it, experiencing tragedy does not have to make you sad at not taking better precautions. In the same vein, wherever it is possible to adopt a better practice to improve your existing lifestyle, you owe it to yourself to really work hard at implementing the practices that can change your life for the better.

The journey with cancer, eye-opening as it was, would still be for naught if I find a way to return to the unhelpful and even harmful lifestyle I used to lead. The experience showed me the strengths that I could always re-ignite when the occasion calls for it and hopefully, the occasion would be one that entails increased productivity in the areas that you have already started improving instead of in weathering events, that may be a result of the continuation of an unhealthy lifestyle.

6. ***Find a safe place to let your emotions loose so you can cope better:***

Emotions and the effect they can have on us human beings are greatly underestimated. Till this day, I believe strongly that my negligence of my emotional state from the time my partner was diagnosed with Alzheimer's played an important role in speeding up the expression of the cancer gene. This claim is not backed up by any kind of scientific evidence however only by conviction and this was all because I never once opened or let my pent-up emotions loose at any point.

I was going through a great deal around that time and this was clear for anyone to see except to me of course. I was walking around, taking on a great deal of responsibility and struggling under all that weight and yet never admitting to needing a channel to release stress occasionally and the result- huge stress ball. It became clear to me that this same pattern of behaviour was not going to cut it at all if I wanted to survive the breast cancer.

From the point my friend altered my approach to thinking about what procedure to go for using his unconventional approach, I realised that I needed to open up more because the way I saw it, I could not always see the best options for myself and getting a second opinion would not hurt as much as it'd help provide an alternative perspective that can, in fact, create a very suitable solution for whatever fix I find myself in. This allowed me to discuss the emotional challenges with the counsellors at the Queensland Cancer Council in a very open way, unlike I usually would and frankly, it was a lifesaver for me on my journey.

7. *Surround yourself with positivity every chance you get:*

This can be tough and almost impossible to do on a personal level and this goes for both healthy individuals and people suffering from terminal and debilitating illnesses. A positive mindset was the best thing that happened to me as I struggled to win the battle against breast cancer and even since the battle is long over, I find that it still serves me well to keep a positive spirit alive. I've now been told I'm the most positive person to have come across. I always see things from a positive outcome.

After my diagnosis, I could not find a single ray of hope and I know now that an important reason I snapped back to reality instead of sinking further into denial was the result of Mezz's gentle presence urging me to act. It wasn't until I was able to drive out of the hospital by myself that I realized how much positivity and clear thinking she had pumped me with.

As I shared before, I was very sceptical about drawing support or any kind of advice from a stranger yet, I was nothing but glad that I had someone like her to draw me out of my stupor. This same thing goes with my male friend that visited me that day as I sat crying and filled with despair.

I discovered the essence of being surrounded by positive thoughts and I also discovered that if the case for me was that I couldn't muster all the positivity myself, it was important that I had people around me who could aid this process for me most of the time. I might've been strong and resilient and choosing to get through every day however none of this would've been possible without the presence of a positive mindset first.

LET ME GET THIS OFF MY CHEST
- COPING WITH BREAST CANCER ALONE *by* JANICE MUIR

Let Me Get This Off My Chest

In the course of coping with cancer alone, I have changed so much, and this goes beyond the change in my looks or the changes my body went through. I discovered so many hidden strengths in me that served as lifesavers in my darkest moments. It was truly a life-altering experience for me. One that I can now say I am grateful for.

The negative emotions that filled me for so long were major obstacles for me and had to be released in as healthy a manner as possible and I had to choose to do this by myself if I planned to make any headway and also heal from cancer. Facing the challenge alone demanded a great deal of resilience from me and I could not be certain that I was up to the task until I started on the path.

They say that you can only connect the dots moving forward and I most definitely agree with these words. I lived one day at a time, unsure that I'd be alive the next day and I kept up a fighting spirit even when, riddled with chemicals, all I could think of was wanting all of this to end.

I struggled to hold onto hope as my treatments commenced and when I woke up to numb feet as a result of my chemo, I had to hope that it would wear off at some point because I could not envisage living the rest of my life with numb feet.

I let go of the negative emotions that burdened me and tried as much as I could to keep my emotions in the clear, positive areas. I was thankful for each triumph that I experienced along my journey because I was aware that it could be so much worse. Sure, I had big dreams and this cancer was delaying my achievements of those dreams yet, it really gave me pause and allowed me to strategize my plans.

I still wanted all the financial stability I could get. I was going to go about it a different way; a way that did not build up so much stress inside my body. There had been cancer once and if I did not take good care, I had a high chance of getting a recurrence and despite my positivity and belief that this would not be the case, I had to work strongly towards it.

Six years after my cancer journey another impact on life occurred. The Big R was in front of me. R = redundancy of employment. Thirty-five years in the Public Sector both Northern Territory and Queensland. The impact of being told your redundant seemed to come and go rather easily as I seemed to manage upheavals in life much easier than before. Whilst I say thank you to Cancer for being a part of my journey I also say thank you to Redundancy as well as this afforded me the chance to take my much-needed rest and even pursue those fields that I really had a passion for. Coming face to face with my mortality, there was really no way I was going to engage in any kind of work that was unfulfilling and this decision has really served me well as I have gradually unfolded the creative parts of me that I've kept locked away in my bid to just fit in and find a stable source of income.

While battling the big C, I had no certainty that I'd survive it and yet, I trudged on regardless of the emotional pain and psychological pain I went through and since 2011, after being cleared of the breast cancer, I've had a better experience at living a fuller life. I could say that I'd been alive up until I was diagnosed with cancer however not to a serious degree. I neglected my health, emotional and psychological well-being in my bid to make ends meet and I wouldn't describe that as truly being alive.

I have found that most of the time, we all require a life-altering event to occur in our lives occasionally, to shake things up and keep us on our toes. Cancer was that shake-up that I experienced. Even though I might've harboured thoughts in the beginning of my journey about the fact that things did not really need to happen that way for me to take care of my affairs better, it was just the pain and now that the pain is behind me, I know better how to ensure that I truly do not need to feel that much pain before I am able to live a healthier, fuller lifestyle.

I'll leave you with this quote that really reflects one of the key lessons in my journey and if you have a life-changing experience like I have, you know that all you can think about is sharing the lessons you've learned with the next person because, in reality, our experiences are the threads that connect us to each other.

The quote is by *Melissa Steginus* and it reads thus,

> *"Ask questions to gain awareness of what's important to you. Then, assess how to implement and prioritize those values in your day and life."*

About Janice Muir

J anice Muir lead a relatively quiet life until being faced with a few of life's adversities. I was strong and gained my true strength to fight and keep the dream alive.

I have witnessed and experienced many life changing events in my lifetime.

2002	Coping and losing my partner with Alzheimer's Dementia.
2006	My own diverse health issues with cervical cancer and breast cancer, 6 months apart.

I have written 2 books to inspire teenagers to find their passion all comes from within. 4 more plots are ready to go.

2012	I was retrenched from 33 yrs in Public Service
2016-17	My world opened to be an online entrepreneur
2018-2019	Loss of both parents in a short space of time

Re Launch; Re View to Re Focus with a Vision to Win. Janice designed a platform to assist the budding new author in helping to assist their book being written. Most of the work being in a process that allows the client to sit back and know that all the work is being done. Janice provides an effective service that is all online, creating your book for you.

Creating an online course presence is in a self-help process will walk you through assisting to write your book.

Life throws challenges to us to help us grow to find a better way to achieve more. Janice shares a way not only to bring about awareness, however, to open your heart to reach inside to find that essence of who you really are.

Everything we want to achieve in life is already within, we must find the resilience to find a way to achieve.

Janice believes that to achieve something you must first believe. And before that it is good that you have a vision of that outcome as well.

For we are all #BornwithaVision2Win. All experiences in my life have helped to create my WHY...

- Make A Difference
- Give back with awareness
- Leave a Legacy

Janice Muir

I Believe I Achieve

**Coach, Mentor,
Book Writing Service – Author**

www.linkedin.com/in/janicemuir

www.facebook.com/AuthorJanMuir

www.facebook.com/HealingThroughWritingJaniceMuir

www.janicemuir.com

www.jancemuir.com/business-card

www.avisiontowin.com

www.thewellusedkey.com

www.janicemuir.com/books

www.janicemuir.com/books#LetMeGetThisOffMyChest

www.janicemuir.com/books#forgetmenot

janicemuir.com